MENTAL DYNAMIC REVIEW

MENTAL SCORES

Heiko Hansen

MENTAL SCORES / Mental Dynamic Review

ISBN: 978-3-7481-6555-2

Production and publishing: Book on Demand GmbH, Norderstedt / Germany

1st edition (2018)

Copyright: Heiko Hansen

MENTAL DYNAMIC REVIEW

MENTAL SCORES

NAME

_____

Season 20___ /___

Table of Contents

If you have passed the MiD Test (Mental Implicit Dynamic: ViQ® / PST®), please enter the following data here:

Name: _____

Shirt nummer _____ Club _____

Season 20___/___ **Date of MiD-Test:** _____

MiD Code (ViQ® / PST®)

My mental implicit priority / First dynamic, z.B. SO.1

Recognation priority (S or A)	Memory- priority (O or P)	Motivation orientation 1/2/3 oder 4

Please enter the characteristic values here:

S	A	O	P	Sti	Sic

www.mentaldynamic.info

MD Profiling

If you would like an evaluation interview with a certified
MD Profiler, then please wear your most important
insights that are important for your sporting mental success!

MD seasonal goals

which I want to achieve or learn/train. Set yourself one season goal each, at most two goals. It's not about the amount of goals, but about the development of meaningful things to constancy.

Tactically

Technically

Athletic

Mentally

This is how I want to perform mentally, act mentally in a game/match or tournament.

My self-responsibility, or rather, I do this on my own commitment in order to play successfully.

That's what I expect from the trainer (team). That's what I need!

Signature Me / Player   **Signature Coach**

© HeikoHansen.de

Important notes

1 / Items

From my more than 25 years of experience, I have defined the most important mental criteria that determine mental performance. Ultimately, it's all about success in the competition and showing your talent and potential in a sustainable way. The feeling of having achieved, if not exceeded, one's performance is another than having failed.

It is primarily about learning success through a fair review: for an attentive, recognizing development and the view of the momentum. And: It's about a basis for discussion and knowledge that should enable the development of mental talent for a successful overall performance.

1a / In consultation between player/athlete and coach, the given criteria can be changed or exchanged and/or up to three additional criteria can be entered. The item "team spirit" should be less interesting for individual athletes.

The item "team spirit" should be less interesting for individual athletes. In golf, for example, the team would be the "4er" and in tennis the "Double".

You can decide for yourself or as a trainer you can specify specific sports, e.g. for GOALKEEPERS like penalty area control, reaction speed etc.

Another reason can be special mental goals for the season, e.g. those resulting from the MiD test or for the mental training of meaning are.

1b / After each match / tournament please enter the **winner item** (best rated) and the **loser item** in the season performance (orange). This gives you a quick overview of your mental strengths and what you still have to work on.

1c / Tactical implementation
Tactical task reliably fulfilled / acting in momentum / behaviour during tactical change / tactical ideas - solutions

1d / Self-activation / power
Energy potential fully exploited / everything given / willingness and joy to perform / pushes oneself (self-talk) / activation in the half-time break or before the game

1e / Focus and concentration
Attention level / sustainable or changing phases

1f / Emotion control
Emotional stability / Creativity - Surprising actions / Dealing with fear or provocation

1g / Fighting Spirit
Two-fight leadership / has fought back / has asserted / acted with courage / effective aggressiveness / opponent - opponent impressed

1h / Competition setting
Self-development of a positive competitive mood / desire Will to win (grade 1 - 2)
or rather fear / scepticism / insecure charisma / stage fright too high (grades 3 - 4)

1i / Action safety
Effectiveness / Cleverness / Decisions made correctly / High self-efficacy / Personal initiative

1j / Mental stability
Mentally strong and stable under pressure / dealing with mistakes and unsuccessful actions / not provocative / good emotion regulation

1k / Body language
Positive charisma / head up / down / expression of self-doubt / giving up

1l / Team spirit
Coached and helped fellow players / Team support such as cheering up, ironing out mistakes made by other players / Corrections made / Direct communication and approaching fellow players

2 / Rating (grades)
For me, notes are a form of evaluation and serve to orient the performance shown. They do not mean the absolute truth. Our sensory perception and evaluation system are too weak for this. Video studies are also helpful accordingly.

Personally I recommend a grading system of 1-2-3-4. The criteria must be clear: when is a 1 a 1, when is a 2 a 2. The grading feeling is different in people, e.g. how strictly one grades.

For orientation I recommend:
Grade 1 is very good and reflects a perfect performance of 90-100% reflected.
Grade 2 between 80-90%.
Grade 3 between 70-80%.
Grade 4 is below 70%.

After internal arrangement you can also between evalua-
tions
in 0.5 steps: 1.5 / 2.5 / 3.5.
1,5 = 95% / 2,5 = 85% / 3,5 = 75%.

3 / Third evaluator

Beside the own evaluation and by the (co-)trainer a third
person should evaluate the mental performance, e.g. parent
part, mental trainer, club scout, consultant or also interesting
a fellow player.

The third person can or should change from game to game.
Therefore, the field for entering the name has remained
white. The third evaluator can be entered alternately. Changing the name makes sense: It can easily lead to a 2:1 opponent ratio. If two evaluators are too critical or uncritical, the
feedback will not achieve the learning goal.

4 / Meaning of the two average grades

4a / On the right the average score of the ratings for the
respective item is noted, e.g. "tactical implementation":
I/player = 2 / Trainer = 1 / 3.evaluator = 2, gives an average
score of 1,67.

4b / The game score must be entered at the bottom. It
results from the average of all items.

5 / NOTE 1

The evaluation approaches are different. You have to
calibrate yourself in the criteria (see note 2). Otherwise it will

quickly lead to discord and misunderstanding between you. Some scorers are too low/pampering, some too high/strict. Some people are more (self-)critical (perfectionists), some are more careless-giving (let five be straight). All the more important is the calibration of the evaluation standards.

Much is gained when the use of this tool leads to more Balance/clarity in the moment, profitable discussions and to more self-responsibility for the own talent development leads. This also applies to the trainer and his own trainer talents.

Let us best follow the path of the shining eyes (pure motivation), curiosity and openness for learning. But you don't have to be able to do everything. Nobody is perfect. Mistakes belong to life and are to be understood as 'helpers'. AND not to forget: There are specialists to support you.

6 / NOTE 2
Please clarify all items and evaluation approaches BEFORE you start the performance evaluation.

7 / NOTE 3
Use this tool seriously and sustainably. All the more success and clarity it will bring.

8 / MENTAL MASTER
To intensify the use of the Mental Dynamic Score, you can choose or award one Mental Master per game/match or tournament, per month and/or per season as a coach/club.

My Season Performance / Mental Scores

GAMES	ME	Coach	3.Person	Winner-Item	Loser-Item
Game 1					
Game 2					
Game 3					
Game 4					
Game 5					
Game 6					
Game 7					
Game 8					
Game 9					
Game 10					
Game 11					
Game 12					
Game 13					
Game 14					
Game 15					
Game 16					
Average					

GAMES	Me	Coach	3.Person	Winner-Item	Loser-Item
Game 17					
Game 18					
Game 19					
Game 20					
Game 21					
Game 22					
Game 23					
Game 24					
Game 25					
Game 26					
Game 27					
Game 28					
Game 29					
Game 30					
Game 31					
Game 32					
Average					

GAMES	Me	Coach	3.Person	Winner-Item	Loser-Item
Game 33					
Game 34					
Game 35					
Game 36					
Game 37					
Game 38					
Game 39					
Game 40					
Game 41					
Game 42					
Game 43					
Game 44					
Game 45					
Game 46					
Game 47					
Game 48					
Average					

Important findings / comments

Goals for the next season

Game / Tournament 1 _____

Date: _____   Play time: _____ H/Min

O League Game   O Cup Game   O International / CL / EL

O Nationalteam   O Practice Game   O Test-/Pre Season Game

Items	Me	Coach		Average
Tactical implementation				
Selfactivating / Power				
Focus / Concentration				
Courageous, self-confident action				
Fighting Spirit				
Competition setting				
Action / handling security				
Mental stability				
Body language				
Team spirit				
Mental Score / Average				

© HeikoHansen.de

Important findings / comments

Goal(s) for the upcoming training week

Goal(s) for the upcoming match/tournament

Game / Tournament 2 _____

Date: _____ Play time: _____ H/Min

○ League Game   ○ Cup Game   ○ International / CL / EL

○ Nationalteam   ○ Practice Game   ○ Test-/Pre Season Game

Items	Me	Coach		Average
Tactical implementation				
Selfactivating / Power				
Focus / Concentration				
Courageous, self-confident action				
Fighting Spirit				
Competition setting				
Action / handling security				
Mental stability				
Body language				
Team spirit				
Mental Score / Average				

Important findings / comments

Goal(s) for the upcoming training week

Goal(s) for the upcoming match/tournament

Game / Tournament 3 _____

Date: _____   Play time: _____ H/Min

O League Game   O Cup Game   O International / CL / EL

O Nationalteam   O Practice Game   O Test-/Pre Season Game

Items	Me	Coach		Average
Tactical implementation				
Selfactivating / Power				
Focus / Concentration				
Courageous, self-confident action				
Fighting Spirit				
Competition setting				
Action / handling security				
Mental stability				
Body language				
Team spirit				
Mental Score / Average				

Important findings / comments

Goal(s) for the upcoming training week

Goal(s) for the upcoming match/tournament

Game / Tournament 4 _____

Date: _____   Play time: _____ H/Min

O League Game   O Cup Game   O International / CL / EL

O Nationalteam   O Practice Game   O Test-/Pre Season Game

Items	Me	Coach		Average
Tactical implementation				
Selfactivating / Power				
Focus / Concentration				
Courageous, self-confident action				
Fighting Spirit				
Competition setting				
Action / handling security				
Mental stability				
Body language				
Team spirit				
Mental Score / Average				

Important findings / comments

Goal(s) for the upcoming training week

Goal(s) for the upcoming match/tournament

Game / Tournament 5 _____

Date: _____   Play time: _____ H/Min

O League Game   O Cup Game   O International / CL / EL

O Nationalteam   O Practice Game   O Test-/Pre Season Game

Items	Me	Coach		Average
Tactical implementation				
Selfactivating / Power				
Focus / Concentration				
Courageous, self-confident action				
Fighting Spirit				
Competition setting				
Action / handling security				
Mental stability				
Body language				
Team spirit				
Mental Score / Average				

© HeikoHansen.de

Important findings / comments

Goal(s) for the upcoming training week

Goal(s) for the upcoming match/tournament

Game / Tournament 6 _____

Date: _____   Play time: _____ H/Min

O League Game   O Cup Game   O International / CL / EL

O Nationalteam   O Practice Game   O Test-/Pre Season Game

Items	Me	Coach		Average
Tactical implementation				
Selfactivating / Power				
Focus / Concentration				
Courageous, self-confident action				
Fighting Spirit				
Competition setting				
Action / handling security				
Mental stability				
Body language				
Team spirit				
Mental Score / Average				

© HeikoHansen.de

Important findings / comments

Goal(s) for the upcoming training week

Goal(s) for the upcoming match/tournament

Game / Tournament 7 _____

Date: _____   Play time: _____ H/Min

O League Game   O Cup Game   O International / CL / EL

O Nationalteam   O Practice Game   O Test-/Pre Season Game

Items	Me	Coach		Average
Tactical implementation				
Selfactivating / Power				
Focus / Concentration				
Courageous, self-confident action				
Fighting Spirit				
Competition setting				
Action / handling security				
Mental stability				
Body language				
Team spirit				
Mental Score / Average				

Important findings / comments

Goal(s) for the upcoming training week

Goal(s) for the upcoming match/tournament

Game / Tournament 8 _____

Date: _____ Play time: _____ H/Min

O League Game   O Cup Game   O International / CL / EL

O Nationalteam   O Practice Game   O Test-/Pre Season Game

Items	Me	Coach		Average
Tactical implementation				
Selfactivating / Power				
Focus / Concentration				
Courageous, self-confident action				
Fighting Spirit				
Competition setting				
Action / handling security				
Mental stability				
Body language				
Team spirit				
Mental Score / Average				

Important findings / comments

Goal(s) for the upcoming training week

Goal(s) for the upcoming match/tournament

Game / Tournament 9 _____

Date: _____   Play time: _____ H/Min

O League Game   O Cup Game   O International / CL / EL

O Nationalteam   O Practice Game   O Test-/Pre Season Game

Items	Me	Coach		Average
Tactical implementation				
Selfactivating / Power				
Focus / Concentration				
Courageous, self-confident action				
Fighting Spirit				
Competition setting				
Action / handling security				
Mental stability				
Body language				
Team spirit				
Mental Score / Average				

Important findings / comments

Goal(s) for the upcoming training week

Goal(s) for the upcoming match/tournament

Game / Tournament 10 _____

Date: _____   Play time: _____ H/Min

O League Game   O Cup Game   O International / CL / EL

O Nationalteam   O Practice Game   O Test-/Pre Season Game

Items	Me	Coach		Average
Tactical implementation				
Selfactivating / Power				
Focus / Concentration				
Courageous, self-confident action				
Fighting Spirit				
Competition setting				
Action / handling security				
Mental stability				
Body language				
Team spirit				
Mental Score / Average				

Important findings / comments

Goal(s) for the upcoming training week

Goal(s) for the upcoming match/tournament

Game / Tournament 11 _____

Date: _____ Play time: _____ H/Min

O League Game   O Cup Game   O International / CL / EL

O Nationalteam   O Practice Game   O Test-/Pre Season Game

Items	Me	Coach		Average
Tactical implementation				
Selfactivating / Power				
Focus / Concentration				
Courageous, self-confident action				
Fighting Spirit				
Competition setting				
Action / handling security				
Mental stability				
Body language				
Team spirit				
Mental Score / Average				

© HeikoHansen.de

Important findings / comments

Goal(s) for the upcoming training week

Goal(s) for the upcoming match/tournament

Game / Tournament 12 _____

Date: _____   Play time: _____ H/Min

O League Game   O Cup Game   O International / CL / EL

O Nationalteam   O Practice Game   O Test-/Pre Season Game

Items	Me	Coach		Average
Tactical implementation				
Selfactivating / Power				
Focus / Concentration				
Courageous, self-confident action				
Fighting Spirit				
Competition setting				
Action / handling security				
Mental stability				
Body language				
Team spirit				
Mental Score / Average				

Important findings / comments

Goal(s) for the upcoming training week

Goal(s) for the upcoming match/tournament

Game / Tournament 13 _____

Date: _____   Play time: _____ H/Min

O League Game   O Cup Game   O International / CL / EL

O Nationalteam   O Practice Game   O Test-/Pre Season Game

Items	Me	Coach		Average
Tactical implementation				
Selfactivating / Power				
Focus / Concentration				
Courageous, self-confident action				
Fighting Spirit				
Competition setting				
Action / handling security				
Mental stability				
Body language				
Team spirit				
Mental Score / Average				

© HeikoHansen.de

Important findings / comments

Goal(s) for the upcoming training week

Goal(s) for the upcoming match/tournament

Game / Tournament 14 _____

Date: _____   Play time: _____ H/Min

O League Game   O Cup Game   O International / CL / EL

O Nationalteam   O Practice Game   O Test-/Pre Season Game

Items	Me	Coach		Average
Tactical implementation				
Selfactivating / Power				
Focus / Concentration				
Courageous, self-confident action				
Fighting Spirit				
Competition setting				
Action / handling security				
Mental stability				
Body language				
Team spirit				
Mental Score / Average				

Important findings / comments

Goal(s) for the upcoming training week

Goal(s) for the upcoming match/tournament

Game / Tournament 15 _____

Date: _____   Play time: _____ H/Min

O League Game   O Cup Game   O International / CL / EL

O Nationalteam   O Practice Game   O Test-/Pre Season Game

Items	Me	Coach		Average
Tactical implementation				
Selfactivating / Power				
Focus / Concentration				
Courageous, self-confident action				
Fighting Spirit				
Competition setting				
Action / handling security				
Mental stability				
Body language				
Team spirit				
Mental Score / Average				

© HeikoHansen.de

Important findings / comments

Goal(s) for the upcoming training week

Goal(s) for the upcoming match/tournament

Game / Tournament 16 _____

Date: _____ Play time: _____ H/Min

O League Game   O Cup Game   O International / CL / EL

O Nationalteam   O Practice Game   O Test-/Pre Season Game

Items	Me	Coach		Average
Tactical implementation				
Selfactivating / Power				
Focus / Concentration				
Courageous, self-confident action				
Fighting Spirit				
Competition setting				
Action / handling security				
Mental stability				
Body language				
Team spirit				
Mental Score / Average				

Important findings / comments

Goal(s) for the upcoming training week

Goal(s) for the upcoming match/tournament

Game / Tournament 17 _____

Date: _____   Play time: _____ H/Min

O League Game   O Cup Game   O International / CL / EL

O Nationalteam   O Practice Game   O Test-/Pre Season Game

Items	Me	Coach		Average
Tactical implementation				
Selfactivating / Power				
Focus / Concentration				
Courageous, self-confident action				
Fighting Spirit				
Competition setting				
Action / handling security				
Mental stability				
Body language				
Team spirit				
Mental Score / Average				

© HeikoHansen.de

Important findings / comments

Goal(s) for the upcoming training week

Goal(s) for the upcoming match/tournament

Game / Tournament 18 _____

Date: _____   Play time: _____ H/Min

O League Game   O Cup Game   O International / CL / EL

O Nationalteam   O Practice Game   O Test-/Pre Season Game

Items	Me	Coach		Average
Tactical implementation				
Selfactivating / Power				
Focus / Concentration				
Courageous, self-confident action				
Fighting Spirit				
Competition setting				
Action / handling security				
Mental stability				
Body language				
Team spirit				
Mental Score / Average				

© HeikoHansen.de

Important findings / comments

Goal(s) for the upcoming training week

Goal(s) for the upcoming match/tournament

Game / Tournament 19 _____

Date: _____   Play time: _____ H/Min

O League Game   O Cup Game   O International / CL / EL

O Nationalteam   O Practice Game   O Test-/Pre Season Game

Items	Me	Coach		Average
Tactical implementation				
Selfactivating / Power				
Focus / Concentration				
Courageous, self-confident action				
Fighting Spirit				
Competition setting				
Action / handling security				
Mental stability				
Body language				
Team spirit				
Mental Score / Average				

Important findings / comments

Goal(s) for the upcoming training week

Goal(s) for the upcoming match/tournament

Game / Tournament 20 _____

Date: _____   Play time: _____ H/Min

O League Game   O Cup Game   O International / CL / EL

O Nationalteam   O Practice Game   O Test-/Pre Season Game

Items	Me	Coach		Average
Tactical implementation				
Selfactivating / Power				
Focus / Concentration				
Courageous, self-confident action				
Fighting Spirit				
Competition setting				
Action / handling security				
Mental stability				
Body language				
Team spirit				
Mental Score / Average				

Important findings / comments

Goal(s) for the upcoming training week

Goal(s) for the upcoming match/tournament

Game / Tournament 21 _____

Date: _____ Play time: _____ H/Min

O League Game   O Cup Game   O International / CL / EL

O Nationalteam   O Practice Game   O Test-/Pre Season Game

Items	Me	Coach		Average
Tactical implementation				
Selfactivating / Power				
Focus / Concentration				
Courageous, self-confident action				
Fighting Spirit				
Competition setting				
Action / handling security				
Mental stability				
Body language				
Team spirit				
Mental Score / Average				

Important findings / comments

Goal(s) for the upcoming training week

Goal(s) for the upcoming match/tournament

Game / Tournament 22 _____

Date: _____   Play time: _____ H/Min

O League Game   O Cup Game   O International / CL / EL

O Nationalteam   O Practice Game   O Test-/Pre Season Game

Items	Me	Coach		Average
Tactical implementation				
Selfactivating / Power				
Focus / Concentration				
Courageous, self-confident action				
Fighting Spirit				
Competition setting				
Action / handling security				
Mental stability				
Body language				
Team spirit				
Mental Score / Average				

© HeikoHansen.de

Important findings / comments

Goal(s) for the upcoming training week

Goal(s) for the upcoming match/tournament

Game / Tournament 23 _____

Date: _____   Play time: _____ H/Min

O League Game   O Cup Game   O International / CL / EL

O Nationalteam   O Practice Game   O Test-/Pre Season Game

Items	Me	Coach		Average
Tactical implementation				
Selfactivating / Power				
Focus / Concentration				
Courageous, self-confident action				
Fighting Spirit				
Competition setting				
Action / handling security				
Mental stability				
Body language				
Team spirit				.
Mental Score / Average				

Important findings / comments

Goal(s) for the upcoming training week

Goal(s) for the upcoming match/tournament

Game / Tournament 24 _____

Date: _____   Play time: _____ H/Min

O League Game   O Cup Game   O International / CL / EL

O Nationalteam   O Practice Game   O Test-/Pre Season Game

Items	Me	Coach		Average
Tactical implementation				
Selfactivating / Power				
Focus / Concentration				
Courageous, self-confident action				
Fighting Spirit				
Competition setting				
Action / handling security				
Mental stability				
Body language				
Team spirit				
Mental Score / Average				

© HeikoHansen.de

Important findings / comments

Goal(s) for the upcoming training week

Goal(s) for the upcoming match/tournament

Game / Tournament 25 _____

Date: _____   Play time: _____ H/Min

O League Game   O Cup Game   O International / CL / EL

O Nationalteam   O Practice Game   O Test-/Pre Season Game

Items	Me	Coach		Average
Tactical implementation				
Selfactivating / Power				
Focus / Concentration				
Courageous, self-confident action				
Fighting Spirit				
Competition setting				
Action / handling security				
Mental stability				
Body language				
Team spirit				
Mental Score / Average				

© HeikoHansen.de

Important findings / comments

Goal(s) for the upcoming training week

Goal(s) for the upcoming match/tournament

Game / Tournament 26 _____

Date: _____   Play time: _____ H/Min

O League Game   O Cup Game   O International / CL / EL

O Nationalteam   O Practice Game   O Test-/Pre Season Game

Items	Me	Coach		Average
Tactical implementation				
Selfactivating / Power				
Focus / Concentration				
Courageous, self-confident action				
Fighting Spirit				
Competition setting				
Action / handling security				
Mental stability				
Body language				
Team spirit				
Mental Score / Average				

© HeikoHansen.de

Important findings / comments

Goal(s) for the upcoming training week

Goal(s) for the upcoming match/tournament

Game / Tournament 27 _____

Date: _____   Play time: _____ H/Min

O League Game   O Cup Game   O International / CL / EL

O Nationalteam   O Practice Game   O Test-/Pre Season Game

Items	Me	Coach		Average
Tactical implementation				
Selfactivating / Power				
Focus / Concentration				
Courageous, self-confident action				
Fighting Spirit				
Competition setting				
Action / handling security				
Mental stability				
Body language				
Team spirit				
Mental Score / Average				

© HeikoHansen.de

Important findings / comments

Goal(s) for the upcoming training week

Goal(s) for the upcoming match/tournament

Game / Tournament 28 _____

Date: _____   Play time: _____ H/Min

O League Game   O Cup Game   O International / CL / EL

O Nationalteam   O Practice Game   O Test-/Pre Season Game

Items	Me	Coach		Average
Tactical implementation				
Selfactivating / Power				
Focus / Concentration				
Courageous, self-confident action				
Fighting Spirit				
Competition setting				
Action / handling security				
Mental stability				
Body language				
Team spirit				
Mental Score / Average				

Important findings / comments

Goal(s) for the upcoming training week

Goal(s) for the upcoming match/tournament

Game / Tournament 29 _____

Date: _____   Play time: _____ H/Min

O League Game   O Cup Game   O International / CL / EL

O Nationalteam   O Practice Game   O Test-/Pre Season Game

Items	Me	Coach		Average
Tactical implementation				
Selfactivating / Power				
Focus / Concentration				
Courageous, self-confident action				
Fighting Spirit				
Competition setting				
Action / handling security				
Mental stability				
Body language				
Team spirit				
Mental Score / Average				

Important findings / comments

Goal(s) for the upcoming training week

Goal(s) for the upcoming match/tournament

Game / Tournament 30 _____

Date: _____   Play time: _____ H/Min

O League Game   O Cup Game   O International / CL / EL

O Nationalteam   O Practice Game   O Test-/Pre Season Game

Items	Me	Coach		Average
Tactical implementation				
Selfactivating / Power				
Focus / Concentration				
Courageous, self-confident action				
Fighting Spirit				
Competition setting				
Action / handling security				
Mental stability				
Body language				
Team spirit				
Mental Score / Average				

Important findings / comments

Goal(s) for the upcoming training week

Goal(s) for the upcoming match/tournament

Game / Tournament 31 _____

Date: _____   Play time: _____ H/Min

O League Game   O Cup Game   O International / CL / EL

O Nationalteam   O Practice Game   O Test-/Pre Season Game

Items	Me	Coach		Average
Tactical implementation				
Selfactivating / Power				
Focus / Concentration				
Courageous, self-confident action				
Fighting Spirit				
Competition setting				
Action / handling security				
Mental stability				
Body language				
Team spirit				
Mental Score / Average				

Important findings / comments

Goal(s) for the upcoming training week

Goal(s) for the upcoming match/tournament

Game / Tournament 32 _____

Date: _____   Play time: _____ H/Min

O League Game   O Cup Game   O International / CL / EL

O Nationalteam   O Practice Game   O Test-/Pre Season Game

Items	Me	Coach		Average
Tactical implementation				
Selfactivating / Power				
Focus / Concentration				
Courageous, self-confident action				
Fighting Spirit				
Competition setting				
Action / handling security				
Mental stability				
Body language				
Team spirit				
Mental Score / Average				

Important findings / comments

Goal(s) for the upcoming training week

Goal(s) for the upcoming match/tournament

Game / Tournament 33 _____

Date: _____   Play time: _____ H/Min

O League Game   O Cup Game   O International / CL / EL

O Nationalteam   O Practice Game   O Test-/Pre Season Game

Items	Me	Coach		Average
Tactical implementation				
Selfactivating / Power				
Focus / Concentration				
Courageous, self-confident action				
Fighting Spirit				
Competition setting				
Action / handling security				
Mental stability				
Body language				
Team spirit				
Mental Score / Average				

© HeikoHansen.de

Important findings / comments

Goal(s) for the upcoming training week

Goal(s) for the upcoming match/tournament

Game / Tournament 34 _____

Date: _____ Play time: _____ H/Min

O League Game   O Cup Game   O International / CL / EL

O Nationalteam   O Practice Game   O Test-/Pre Season Game

Items	Me	Coach		Average
Tactical implementation				
Selfactivating / Power				
Focus / Concentration				
Courageous, self-confident action				
Fighting Spirit				
Competition setting				
Action / handling security				
Mental stability				
Body language				
Team spirit				
Mental Score / Average				

Important findings / comments

Goal(s) for the upcoming training week

Goal(s) for the upcoming match/tournament

Game / Tournament 35 _____

Date: _____   Play time: _____ H/Min

O League Game   O Cup Game   O International / CL / EL

O Nationalteam   O Practice Game   O Test-/Pre Season Game

Items	Me	Coach		Average
Tactical implementation				
Selfactivating / Power				
Focus / Concentration				
Courageous, self-confident action				
Fighting Spirit				
Competition setting				
Action / handling security				
Mental stability				
Body language				
Team spirit				
Mental Score / Average				

Important findings / comments

Goal(s) for the upcoming training week

Goal(s) for the upcoming match/tournament

Game / Tournament 36 _____

Date: _____ Play time: _____ H/Min

O League Game   O Cup Game   O International / CL / EL

O Nationalteam   O Practice Game   O Test-/Pre Season Game

Items	Me	Coach		Average
Tactical implementation				
Selfactivating / Power				
Focus / Concentration				
Courageous, self-confident action				
Fighting Spirit				
Competition setting				
Action / handling security				
Mental stability				
Body language				
Team spirit				
Mental Score / Average				

Important findings / comments

Goal(s) for the upcoming training week

Goal(s) for the upcoming match/tournament

Game / Tournament 37 _____

Date: _____ Play time: _____ H/Min

O League Game   O Cup Game   O International / CL / EL

O Nationalteam   O Practice Game   O Test-/Pre Season Game

Items	Me	Coach		Average
Tactical implementation				
Selfactivating / Power				
Focus / Concentration				
Courageous, self-confident action				
Fighting Spirit				
Competition setting				
Action / handling security				
Mental stability				
Body language				
Team spirit				
Mental Score / Average				

Important findings / comments

Goal(s) for the upcoming training week

Goal(s) for the upcoming match/tournament

Game / Tournament 38 _____

Date: _____   Play time: _____ H/Min

O League Game   O Cup Game   O International / CL / EL

O Nationalteam   O Practice Game   O Test-/Pre Season Game

Items	Me	Coach		Average
Tactical implementation				
Selfactivating / Power				
Focus / Concentration				
Courageous, self-confident action				
Fighting Spirit				
Competition setting				
Action / handling security				
Mental stability				
Body language				
Team spirit				
Mental Score / Average				

Important findings / comments

Goal(s) for the upcoming training week

Goal(s) for the upcoming match/tournament

Game / Tournament 39 _____

Date: _____   Play time: _____ H/Min

O League Game   O Cup Game   O International / CL / EL

O Nationalteam   O Practice Game   O Test-/Pre Season Game

Items	Me	Coach		Average
Tactical implementation				
Selfactivating / Power				
Focus / Concentration				
Courageous, self-confident action				
Fighting Spirit				
Competition setting				
Action / handling security				
Mental stability				
Body language				
Team spirit				
Mental Score / Average				

Important findings / comments

Goal(s) for the upcoming training week

Goal(s) for the upcoming match/tournament

Game / Tournament 40 _____

Date: _____   Play time: _____ H/Min

O League Game   O Cup Game   O International / CL / EL

O Nationalteam   O Practice Game   O Test-/Pre Season Game

Items	Me	Coach		Average
Tactical implementation				
Selfactivating / Power				
Focus / Concentration				
Courageous, self-confident action				
Fighting Spirit				
Competition setting				
Action / handling security				
Mental stability				
Body language				
Team spirit				
Mental Score / Average				

Important findings / comments

Goal(s) for the upcoming training week

Goal(s) for the upcoming match/tournament

Game / Tournament 41 _____

Date: _____   Play time: _____ H/Min

O League Game   O Cup Game   O International / CL / EL

O Nationalteam   O Practice Game   O Test-/Pre Season Game

Items	Me	Coach		Average
Tactical implementation				
Selfactivating / Power				
Focus / Concentration				
Courageous, self-confident action				
Fighting Spirit				
Competition setting				
Action / handling security				
Mental stability				
Body language				
Team spirit				
Mental Score / Average				

Important findings / comments

Goal(s) for the upcoming training week

Goal(s) for the upcoming match/tournament

Game / Tournament 42 _____

Date: _____   Play time: _____ H/Min

O League Game   O Cup Game   O International / CL / EL

O Nationalteam   O Practice Game   O Test-/Pre Season Game

Items	Me	Coach		Average
Tactical implementation				
Selfactivating / Power				
Focus / Concentration				
Courageous, self-confident action				
Fighting Spirit				
Competition setting				
Action / handling security				
Mental stability				
Body language				
Team spirit				
Mental Score / Average				

© HeikoHansen.de

Important findings / comments

Goal(s) for the upcoming training week

Goal(s) for the upcoming match/tournament

Game / Tournament 43 _____

Date: _____   Play time: _____ H/Min

O League Game   O Cup Game   O International / CL / EL

O Nationalteam   O Practice Game   O Test-/Pre Season Game

Items	Me	Coach		Average
Tactical implementation				
Selfactivating / Power				
Focus / Concentration				
Courageous, self-confident action				
Fighting Spirit				
Competition setting				
Action / handling security				
Mental stability				
Body language				
Team spirit				
Mental Score / Average				

Important findings / comments

Goal(s) for the upcoming training week

Goal(s) for the upcoming match/tournament

Game / Tournament 44 _____

Date: _____   Play time: _____ H/Min

O League Game   O Cup Game   O International / CL / EL

O Nationalteam   O Practice Game   O Test-/Pre Season Game

Items	Me	Coach		Average
Tactical implementation				
Selfactivating / Power				
Focus / Concentration				
Courageous, self-confident action				
Fighting Spirit				
Competition setting				
Action / handling security				
Mental stability				
Body language				
Team spirit				
Mental Score / Average				

Important findings / comments

Goal(s) for the upcoming training week

Goal(s) for the upcoming match/tournament

Game / Tournament 45 _____

Date: _____   Play time: _____ H/Min

O League Game   O Cup Game   O International / CL / EL

O Nationalteam   O Practice Game   O Test-/Pre Season Game

Items	Me	Coach		Average
Tactical implementation				
Selfactivating / Power				
Focus / Concentration				
Courageous, self-confident action				
Fighting Spirit				
Competition setting				
Action / handling security				
Mental stability				
Body language				
Team spirit				
Mental Score / Average				

Important findings / comments

Goal(s) for the upcoming training week

Goal(s) for the upcoming match/tournament

Game / Tournament 46 _____

Date: _____   Play time: _____ H/Min

O League Game   O Cup Game   O International / CL / EL

O Nationalteam   O Practice Game   O Test-/Pre Season Game

Items	Me	Coach		Average
Tactical implementation				
Selfactivating / Power				
Focus / Concentration				
Courageous, self-confident action				
Fighting Spirit				
Competition setting				
Action / handling security				
Mental stability				
Body language				
Team spirit				
Mental Score / Average				

Important findings / comments

Goal(s) for the upcoming training week

Goal(s) for the upcoming match/tournament

Game / Tournament 47 _____

Date: _____   Play time: _____ H/Min

O League Game   O Cup Game   O International / CL / EL

O Nationalteam   O Practice Game   O Test-/Pre Season Game

Items	Me	Coach		Average
Tactical implementation				
Selfactivating / Power				
Focus / Concentration				
Courageous, self-confident action				
Fighting Spirit				
Competition setting				
Action / handling security				
Mental stability				
Body language				
Team spirit				
Mental Score / Average				

Important findings / comments

Goal(s) for the upcoming training week

Goal(s) for the upcoming match/tournament

Game / Tournament 48 _____

Date: _____ Play time: _____ H/Min

O League Game   O Cup Game   O International / CL / EL

O Nationalteam   O Practice Game   O Test-/Pre Season Game

Items	Me	Coach		Average
Tactical implementation				
Selfactivating / Power				
Focus / Concentration				
Courageous, self-confident action				
Fighting Spirit				
Competition setting				
Action / handling security				
Mental stability				
Body language				
Team spirit				
Mental Score / Average				

Important findings / comments

Goal(s) for the upcoming training week

Goal(s) for the upcoming match/tournament

NOTICE